T0114696

# WHY DOES ART EDUCATION MATTER?

ZARTASHA SHAH

authorHOUSE·

*AuthorHouse™*
*1663 Liberty Drive*
*Bloomington, IN 47403*
*www.authorhouse.com*
*Phone: 833-262-8899*

*Published by AuthorHouse  07/12/2023*

*ISBN: 979-8-8230-1134-1 (sc)*
*ISBN: 979-8-8230-1133-4 (e)*

*Library of Congress Control Number: 2023912528*

*Print information available on the last page.*

*This book is printed on acid-free paper.*

To my family, friends, instructors, students, well-wishers, and the art education lovers!

# INTRODUCTION

This book revolves around my life's inspirations, teachings, learnings, knowledge, observations, and experiences. Art education has changed perspectives in multiple ways and makes me think more uniquely than the previous years. Now, this is a way to support the process of implementation, interpretation, collaboration, and amplification in it. This experience also has informed me about the importance of the interpersonal, instructional, and sustainable development of learnings in education and these learnings and teachings will last forever!

Zartasha Shah

# CONTENTS

# A VISUAL CULTURE-BASED ART EDUCATION IN EDUCATION

History of art education and a historical approach in a visual culture-based art education revolve around the theory of art education and inform about having an impact on others through several skills including social, communicational, and social perspective skills in education. By looking at the details, we can see that the process of learning was started in the learning environment of the United States the Independence of the country. An American visual culture was introduced in the 1800s. The process of learning a historical approach in a visual culture-based art education was also started at the same time.

Art education is able to share the details of the process of making artworks, methods, and the materials of them.

1

For example, pointed arches, flying buttresses, and the rose windows do share the details of their Gothic era with us. The use of the handmade Medieval Manuscripts for the Missal, Chants, daily prayers, occasional prayers, and the Islamic prayers make the artworks more meaningful to us. They do talk about the importance of the artworks for the Christians, Jews, and the Muslims. The Christian mosaics and the Islamic calligraphy of Hagia Sophia, Sistine Chapel's Ceiling and the use of the religious stories for the Ceiling, and the several other valuable artworks do talk about the Renaissance era.

When we look at Emile Zola's writings, especially his novel Nana, we see the details of the Impressionists and the artist of the era, because his work as an art history writer talks about the quality of the artworks of them. When we look at Caravaggio's works with the bright human figures that have the face expressions on their faces, the detailed artworks inspire us. The Edger Degas's Impressionism and work for the artists to support the artists shares the details of his work to us. His inventions, including the fixative and the oil pastels for the ballet dancers do share the information about his interest in the gestures, movement, and the drapery folds in his artworks.

The works of Mary Cassette, Barbara Hepworth, John Singer Sargent, James Montgomery Flagg, David Smith, and Jeff are considerable evidence for the development in the world of art and art history as well.

The implementation, amplification, interpretation, and an evaluation can expand the knowledge for the learners in the several ways. You can use the five ways to be more creative in your everyday life. For example, you can use your imagination, aesthetic sense, genuine style, processes, and the materials to make the artworks more meaningful for you. We do know that the function of an artwork and the colors of affluence can also convey a message to others. Art education has always shared the details of making the artworks and the use of the materials, enactment, advancement, and clarification can make the artworks more meaningful in the several possible ways.

World War I started in 1914 and the war ended in 1918. World War II started in 1939 and the war ended in 1945. In those days, a few people were able to teach art education in education. In the 1960s, art education was introduced as a subject and a few people were able to accept teaching positions in education. It was introduced as a master's and Doctorate major after those years. The response was good, and the graduate students were able to do their research to complete their degree requirements for them. After the offers of a historical approach in a visual culture-based art education, history of art education, art history, studio arts and architecture, and archeology, several institutions offered leadership, curriculum, and instructional education.

In 1982, Discipline-based art education or DBAE

was started, and the National Art Education Association was introduced in 1947. The Government of the United States has helped the department of education by giving a financial and a moral support to make the things possible to the people of the country. The federal government's role in supporting art education informs that the Department of Education has explained the importance of art education through the details of the availability of art education courses as a part of the education curriculum. The importance of art education informs about the use of possible ways to make the planning for the development works in education.

Organizational skills also revolve around the same methods for the product to achieve the goals of integration to support the essential work by art education in education. The research informs us about the importance of implementation, interpretation, education, and information, and helps apply its planning. The official planning of the country has supported the social and educational needs of learners. This also suggests that we need to find ways to make teaching and learning work for learners of art education by using the curriculum and the various levels of teaching in the schools. Information about the use and effectiveness of these efforts, plans, and works to support art education are needed in it. Art education supports learnings educationally, culturally, politically, and socially in the learning environment of education.

President John F. Kennedy introduced an educational program for the independent school districts. No Child Left Behind was introduced in 2001 by President George Bush to support the use of the art education curriculum in education. Problem Solving has an association with the process of using extensive ideas to decide the theme for an artwork. It has no concern with the elements of art and the principles of design. Knowledge base art education is more about the use of the development of lofty ideas to explore new worlds for students. It has no concern with the process of using the latest digital devices, methods, and materials for them.

Personal connections are needed to make the superior quality of an artwork for a student in the classroom. Boundaries have an association with the limits, choices, preferences, and the themes of a student who is willing to create an artwork for him in the learning environment of an institution. Working methods revolve around taking a risk to play and experiment with the multiple things in the classrooms. The use of a curriculum for learners of art education is needed in the curriculum, and distinct levels of teaching are also required for them.

The teachers must use these steps to improve the quality of the artworks of their students by working with their students in the classrooms. An application of art educational theories has an association with the diverse culture, curriculum, and the use of the multiple strategies to make the art education more effective in the learning environment of the country. Art educators must be able to amplify art education properly to get a better result out of it. The importance of art education, art history, visual culture, historical aspects of art history, and a critical review of the visual culture revolves around multiple fields of art including art education, studio art, visual and performing art, social and the cultural aspects of art, art history, and an importance of the accepted curriculum in art education.

An implementation of art education must expand the knowledge of the students by giving them a chance to use their own creativity, aesthetics, and ideology. An interpretation and a collaboration of the educators with the communities, and the use of the communicational and the social skills can help in developing the art teaching skills with the learning process of the students to establish a good relationship between the students and the art educators and the performances of both in art education. The primary emphasis among art educators in dealing with visual culture is to consider the relationship between imagery and the student viewer.

Culture is the best way to educate, inform, and assist about the values of a nation, community, and cultural heritage in education. The art educators need to have an impact on their learners by using the contemporary approach to expand the horizon of the knowledge of the students in the classrooms. Social perspectives including a cultural impact, social skills, and communicational skills are also particularly important in art education. They also support the learning process of the students by giving them a chance to learn more in education.

The art educators do want their students to learn more about the latest technology and the different devices at the schools. The availability of the production and the response of the users can be effective. The response of the users or the viewers can tell the success of the application of these things in the system. The importance of the field of art education and visual culture has an association with social interpretation. The historical background of each artwork is able to convey a message to the readers through the use of materials, methods, and process of creativity in it. It is establishing a good connection though art education by introducing the new things in the system. The outcomes are really good.

Now, the system needs to pay attention to the importance of the curriculum in education. The studio arts, art education, and art history are immensely popular in the system. Most art educators do not want to use any contemporary art styles in their classrooms. They want their students to learn about the seven elements of the arts, the seven principles of design, and the history of art. They also want to use old methods, materials, and techniques to make the artworks in the art rooms. The curriculum is also limiting the knowledge and the creativity of the students. They are required to follow the provided instructions to get a better grade in the art room. If they follow the provided instructions, they can make their well-managed artworks. If the art educators allow their students to make something on their own, the students will use their own creativity, aesthetics, and ideology to create their artworks independently by themselves. The process of learning will develop their own knowledge through the process of making the artworks. The process of making the artwork revolves around the visual culture. The process of deconstruction can also expand the knowledge of the students, therefore; the art educators want their students to learn more through these experiences in the learning environment of education.

Teaching art is a big responsibility and art teachers do accept these challenges to set higher standards of art education in visual culture at their institutions. The process of making the artworks can share the information of the curriculum and the requirements of making artworks in the classes. The use of strategies, concepts, and aesthetics can improve the quality of the artworks. The diverse culture of the United States can become a part of it. The use of the methods and the materials can also affect the representation and the style of the artworks. The process of making the artworks can help students in establishing their relationship and an understanding with their art teachers. The process can inform that students are able to create anything because they are willing to learn in the art rooms. They come into the art room to sit in with their table partners to create something new in the art room.

Ongoing and happening are two different things and they do not go together. When something happens in the art room, students can get help from their teachers. To learn from their art teacher, they are required to follow the classroom rules. To have a good impact on others through the use of the several skills including social, communicational, and social perspective skills in the process of making artworks can support the process of making the artworks in the United States. The hidden meanings behind the artworks can inform about the history of the process of making these artworks by themselves.

The viewers need to dig for the details. The hidden meanings can also hide the knowledge of the artists and the representation of the artworks can still convey a message to the viewers by themselves. The outcomes will be exceptionally good. Therefore, the students are required to learn about the basic techniques of the artworks, and they do need to know about the history of Art Education and a historical approach in a visual culture-based art education in the United States. They just need to use their own creativity to work without putting pressure on them. They also need to know the importance of art in education.

A historical approach in a visual culture-based art education is also valuable in this situation. Social perspectives on art education can expand the knowledge of the readers through the provided details of these things to them.

From my perspective, the provided evidence can share the information about the importance of art history, art education, visual cultural studies, and an application of each of these topics in the system in a chronological order. This chronological order helps to understand the event in an order. For example, the Renaissance era revolves around the early renaissance, high renaissance, northern renaissance, and mannerism. Visual culture is the reflection of its own period of time. I would like to add the headdresses, staffs, and wearable objects of the Americas, Oceania, and African culture in it. The details can tell us that their females were using their wearable objects, headdresses, and staffs to show their ranks and positions to others. It seems that visual culture has an association with both, and this includes the traditional and the nontraditional art and the visual cultural studies about it.

An application of art educational theories has an association with the diverse culture, curriculum, and the use of the multiple strategies to make the art education more effective in the learning environment of the country and the roles of the students and the teachers are particularly important in this situation. The importance of the field of art education and visual culture can talk about the social interpretation and the historical background of each artwork to convey a message to the readers. A historical approach in a visual culture-based art education, social perspectives on art education, and discipline-based art education can share the information about the importance of art history, art education, and visual cultural studies in a chronological order. We can expand the horizon by adding more things to it. The process of making artworks helps in understanding the needs of creativity, aesthetics, and artistic mindedness. The process also develops an interest in the history of the chosen process, and the use of methods, and materials to understand the function of artworks in it.

In the field of education, the use of policies, plans, and federal laws supports the educational environment to update, unify, and make it influential in it. This essential information has informed us about the government entities supporting the NCLB work process in education. The purpose is to support and promote students who need to make timely progress in their classrooms and are supposed to be getting evaluated at the school.

A detailed curriculum plans to keep learning and chosen teaching methods for them. The process of keeping the diverse environment of each classroom helps to teach the curriculum in education. To see learners' progress in the art education classes at the schools, the act can be checked to see the official support for art education in the classrooms. The Department of Education has informed us about the importance of the curriculum.

The use of curriculum makes the process of learning work for learners and shows students' interest in art education. This informs us that a qualified art teacher must demonstrate, explain, and teach art education to support observations, experience, learning, and training of learners. Art education can be a part of education at all levels of education to explain the basic needs of art education. Each individual can support cultural heritage in education. Individual identity is essential, and valuable, and must not be able to support racism. Students can be checked by their personal identities. These issues revolve around separating identities, differences in-between ethnic groups, and racism in education. Therefore, To support art education, the differences in-between students must not be highlighted in education.

The teachers can support cultural identification. Individuality must not make the distances between them. These distances can start a cold relationship to impact the diverse environment of education. To establish social contact with peers, the social norms, social contacts, and social identification must be taken care of by the learners. The whole entire process must be consistent, logical, and meaningful to work for them. The environment of the classes must be engaging, innovative, and inclusive for learners. This information has informed us about students' equal rights and responsibilities in education. Therefore, teachers need to find ways to work with students in it.

Cultural identity informs us about the use and effectiveness of the different methods of teaching individual identification to inform about the personal identification of each individual in it. In an urban educational environment, each individual is willing to show his or her individuality, which may or may not have a good impact on others. Learners often support their own cultural heritage and do not like to spend much time on the details of others unless they have to work on a project for them.

Art educators do like to use their personal choices, preferences, and the accepted terms to make the teachings work for learners in the art rooms and effectiveness of the different teaching methods to inform about the personal identification of each individual learner in it. In an urban educational environment, each individual may or may not have a good impact on others, but they support their own cultural heritage. Each individual learner supports personal identity to support cultural heritage. This must not support the differences between cultural heritage, beliefs, and social norms. Therefore, teachers can support togetherness. The different methods in urban educational environments and interest of educators, impact of individuality, and its cultural heritage can inform about the importance of these things in education.

Each individual's personal identity is essential in education. Each individual learner is willing to show his or her personal identity to support cultural heritage. This also supports multiculturalism, urban art education, and critical race theory. The teachers support the diverse educational environment of the classroom to keep the environment more engaging, innovative, and inclusive in it. This must not support the difference between cultural heritage, beliefs, and social norms. Therefore, teachers need to spend more time explaining the importance of togetherness to them. The research will inform more about the use and effectiveness of the different teaching methods. In an urban educational environment, each individual is willing to show his or her individuality, which may or may not have a good impact on others. Learners often support their own cultural heritage and do not like to spend much time on the details of others unless they have to work on a project for them.

Cultural inquiry is a way to inform the experiences, observations, and learnings to make the process of creativity, aesthetics, and artistic mindedness work for the artists. The best practices for supporting inquiry in art education can help through lived experience, observations, and learnings in education. The best practices for supporting inquiry in art education can help through lived experience, observations, and learnings in education. Using these essential parts of their lives can make the quality of artworks more meaningful, functional, and valuable for others. Therefore, the classroom environment must be inclusive, engaging, and innovative to support multiculturalism in urban institutions. This can support urban learning in urban education. This process can share the details of the methods, themes, and ideas reflected through creativity in education.

The process also can highlight the essential parts of teaching to indicate, inform, and explain the important parts of it, which can keep the entire work transparent in education. experiences, observations, and learnings can make the process of creativity, aesthetics, and artistic mindedness work for the artists. The best practices show the value of using lived experience, observations, and learnings in education. Using these essential parts of lived experiences can make the quality of artworks more meaningful, functional, and valuable. Therefore, the classroom environment must be inclusive, engaging, and innovative to support multiculturalism in urban institutions. This can support urban learning in urban education. This process can share the details of the methods, themes, and ideas that are reflected through creativity in education. The process of the use of methods of teaching indicates, informs, and explains the essential parts of it.

# ADULT LEARNING AND PROFESSIONAL DEVELOPMENT ISSUES OF CURRICULUM IN ART EDUCATION

ADULT LEARNING AND professional development issues of curriculum are noticeable in art education. The teachers are expected to develop their knowledge, skills, and abilities to support the process of implementation for this purpose. They are required to complete their training to make the curriculum work in education. Formal learning revolves around the use of formal ways in classes. The informal or unofficial ways inform us about the use of ordinary ways to support learning. Each learner is supposed to be able to get some help for his or her finances, mental health, and moral support in education.

The adult learning and professional development issues

of curriculum are associated with the lifelong learning in art education. Therefore, the learners are supposed to be able to get the required professional training to learn more in it. A detailed, useful, and an effective lesson plan is needed in the classes. This process can help in understanding the important parts of the required works for them. After the completion of the training, a professional change must be visible in the teachers. Professional identification is an important part of the lifelong learning process for it. The teachers do have the leading roles in education. The behavior of each teacher is able to have an impact on each learner in the classes. The process learnings do helps in managing the behaviors to work in the diverse environment of education. The training revolves around the use of art education curriculum, ability to explain the nature of each assignment to support the creativity, aesthetics, and artistic mindedness for them. They also need to walk around to answer the questions, discuss the plannings, and they need to explain the details of each part of the assignments to their learners.

Financial issues often impact on the professional programs of teachers. They do not let the teachers have access to all of the resources to use to make the quality of education work for them. Adult learning theory revolves around cognitivism, and this can be used to observe the learning abilities of students by using reading material to check the memorization skills of students in education.

The explanation of the importance of reading skills can be discussed in education. The application of the cognitivism theory's concepts can be checked by asking a couple of questions related to their reading in education. The teachings can be investigated by offering an activity in the classroom. The production can be checked by walking around and asking about the favorite parts of the activity in class. The evaluation process can give a chance to see the outcomes by passing out a questionnaire and collecting it from them. Humanistic theory is an important part of education.

We can see that the three philosophers have supported humanistic theory in education. Carl Rogers's humanistic theory work informs that therapeutic relationships can show the negativity in human behaviors in education. Unconditional positivity supports the humanistic theory in education. Abraham Maslow's humanistic theory supports the importance of personal growth in education. To have the desire to learn more to become a prominenet person in the system, people do need to make the efforts to achieve their goals in their lives. James Frederick Thomas Bugental's theory has informed about the lived experiences to have the realities of lives instead of living on the phenomenon. Therefore, the teachers are expected to develop their knowledge, skills, and abilities to make the teachings work effectively in education.

# SOCIAL JUSTICE
# ART EDUCATION

Social justice is more about the importance of social dimension (social interactions, social practice, and social interfaces), self-awareness (moral ethics, authenticity, and aesthetics), and inclusion (public space, intervention, and interface). In the field of art education, this process allows ethnic students to use their aesthetics, artistic mindedness, and creativity for them. This process also makes the learning work through the use of personal knowledge, skills, and abilities in it. The ethnic students are not allowed to use their gender, race, color, religion, and individual identity to get any preference in education. The process of learning is multi-dimensional and revolves around the social communications, social practice, and social norms in it.

The process helps to develop self-awareness, self-confidence, and self-expression in the learning process of them. The social dimensions are about social interactions, social practice, social interfaces, and give a chance to the students to share their influences through their artworks in their classrooms. Self-awareness gives a chance to share personal choices and preferences through the creativity of the art of them. The process of making artworks expands the horizon of knowledge and allows students to learn through the process in it. This process allows students to create their artworks by working independently to show their individuality in their classes. The teachers always like to use their knowledge, skills, and abilities to teach in their classes for them. The process consists of several parts to use to assess, analyze, check, and evaluate the quality of the artworks of their students in it; the critical analysis allows the teachers to check the quality of the artworks by assessing the artworks critically for them.

The social dimensions are about social interactions, social practice, and the social interfaces in social justice art education. Social justice gives a chance to students to share their influences through their artworks and diversity on the equal basis supports the customs, cultures, traditions, values, and the languages in the social justice art education. As an individual, an artist can produce different themes to represent personal identity, individuality, and interactions in multiple ways. We can include social involvement in social justice art education to have a good impact on others, and to convey messages to others by making meaningful and modern artworks for it. The students have to share their ideas, plans, and the methods to use for the creation of the artworks; the chosen themes can help students explore new worlds through the process of making the artworks for them.

Self-awareness can allow students to show their own choices and preferences by themselves. It is always good to know and understand the importance of the use of creativity, aesthetics, and artistic mindedness for them. Therefore, it is important for the art teachers to support students by providing them with instructions so they can use their creativity for them. Self-awareness supports the qualities of the artworks of students by supporting their social and moral ethics, work with fellow artists, team leadership, self-expression, knowledge, skills, and the abilities in education.

Students do need to get their public space to share their own knowledge, skills, and abilities with others. Public space gives a chance to students to make comments, share critical thoughts, and decisions about their own artworks for them. In public schools, the art educators do talk about the importance of public space for students in education. The public space also gives a chance to students to share the space for their educational purposes in education. This allows to show individual identification by occupying a public space so the visitors can physically interact with the artworks.

The function of each artwork changes the value in society. Visual learning helps in understanding the use of methods, materials, techniques, and themes to visitors. The process always helps in establishing a social connection for the visitors with artists. The repercussions are supposed to be understandable, meaningful, and they are also supposed to be functioning as useful artworks in it. The strategies and the approaches are also supposed to be understandable for others. Cultural, educational, and economic issues are especially important in it. We will be able to see less racial issues, less cultural issues, and less global issues in education in the future. Through the (re)contextualization of art, the students can produce their own ideas to implement, amplify, build, reconstruct, rearrange, and present in their own ways for them. The process of teaching training supports teaching skills in multiple ways. They do learn about the importance of teaching methods through project-based learning, object-based learning, and student-based learning in education.

The teachers do learn, practice, and apply their knowledge, skills, and abilities in their classes. They do want to incorporate the learnings in their own ways by using their own methods of teaching to expand the knowledge of the students in the classrooms. The process of teaching must be consistent, logical, and meaningful for learners; the impacts of teachings can expand the knowledge in the learning environment of education. A comprehensive environment is essentially important, inspirational, and innovative in education. This process has to support social, moral, and ethical inspirations and also has to keep the environment more engaging, inclusive, and innovative in education.

# URBAN ART EDUCATION

URBAN EDUCATION REVOLVES around interdisciplinary studies (cross-disciplinary and multi-disciplinary), instructional moves, and behaviorism. This process informs that they have to use the different disciplinary methods to make teachings work for them. This is associated with the values of customs, cultures, traditions, and the cultural heritage in it. They have to plan to implement, interpret, educate, and inform others. The social, cultural, educational, financial, and political issues do impact on the methods of teachings; therefore, the process must be able to indicate, inform, and transparent for it. This can help to keep others connected, engaged, and motivated in it.

The use of curriculum, policies, and procedures help in making the learnings work through the use of theories, practices, and applications of these things in the urban educational environment of the larger cities.

In the field of education, the use of policies, plans, and processes can support learners in the classroom. Using federal laws to keep the educational environment updated, unified, and influential helps support learnings for this purpose. This process can help in keeping the educational environment more inclusive, engaging, and innovative in it. Urban education is also about diversity, equity, and inclusion in education. Urban education talks about the issues, concerns, and the outcomes of social justice in education. The ethnic students are especially important in the system and each student represents his/her personal identification in it. The customs, cultures, traditions, values, and the religions of the ethnic students support the personal identification of each student of them. Social justice also talks about social involvement, social and emotional learning, and social equality. The process of the implementations, interpretations, collaborations, and the evaluations have impacts on the lives of the students in urban education. Interpersonal, intrapersonal, and cognitive strategies also impact their lives.

The history talks about the several philosophers that had supported the basic thoughts of social justice in their lives. For example, Plato was a philosopher of Greece, and the role of the society was always unbelievably valuable in urban education for him. Aristotle was a philosopher of Greek and he informed that the people do need to accept the rules and the regulations of the community to survive in their lives. Socrates was a philosopher of Greek and he informed that the civic duties of the civil society require the people to construct, consider, and collaborate to work together as community. Confucius was a philosopher of China and he had also supported social justice to give a moral support the humanity. John Dewey was a philosopher of America. Therefore, his ideology had worked for the people in multiple ways in urban education. Multicultural students do face the several problems for several reasons in urban education. They have to adapt to the culture of the other ethnic students by communicating with them. The language barriers also affect communicational skills, and this issue does not let the students established their social, cultural, and educational contacts with other students in urban education. The teachers do take the responsibility to support the students by helping in the classrooms with the assignments, research, and the other educational activities of them.

The teachers do not give preferences to their students by ethnicity. The use of the resources including the technology, school supplies, and the internet also impact on the learning process of them. The use of electronic devices helps in conducting research, saving the works, and presenting the research in education. The use of the different browsers, devices, programming, and websites expands the knowledge of the students every day. Lacking resources impact on the academics of the students and financial funding are some of the big reasons behind them. The lack of federal, state, and local funding cannot support the learning process in urban education. The lack of trained teachers affects the progress of the students in education. Therefore, to instruct the students in the urban settings, trained and knowledgeable teachers are needed in the classrooms for the students to expand their knowledge of them. The behavior of students' effect on the values of the living society that requires the unity and an integrity from them.

The teachers do understand that the assignments, core curriculum, theory, and the practice for the students must be completed in a timely manner by the students; they do not need to ignore the importance of them. The process of interpretation supports the implementation of the ideas by finding ways to improve the quality of the works in the system and the students need to incorporate the teaching methods in the learning environment of the education. Urban education is about diversity, equity, inclusion, issues, concerns, and the effects of social justice in education. The ethnic students and their personal identification are important in urban education.

Interpersonal, intrapersonal, and cognitive strategies do have good impacts on them. People do need to accept the rules and the regulation of the community to survive in urban education. For the civic duties of the civil society, people do need to construct, consider, and collaborate to work tother. The teachers need to take the responsibility for the students by considering students their first priority and also by lettering students come to class to learn something new every day at the school. To instruct the ethnic students, the teachers have to improve the quality of the education to keep the classrooms more inclusive and engaging for them.

Urban art education also supports multiculturalism, critical thinking, and visual literacy in education. Multiculturalism is about diversity, cultural heritage, and tradition in education. This diversity is having a good impact on them. When we talk about racism, this situation changes the atmosphere of educational institutions and turns the environment of schools into a racial protest place for them. The outcomes will be able to share the details of the positive changes in the educational environment of urban education.

Visual literacy helps in understanding the details by visually looking at an artwork to learn more through visual literacy, visual learning, and also to understand the visual development of artwork in it. Visual literacy is more about physical appearance, dimensions, and visual learning in an urban environment of education. Visual literacy, social engagement, and having the ability to know and understand the use and function of an artwork are important in education. Therefore, public awareness is about the process of learning visually to inform the use of aesthetics, artistic mindedness, and creativity in education. The importance of social justice in urban art education informs about the important parts of each section of this research including the details of social justice, urban art education, multiculturalism, critical thinking, visual literacy, and the importance of individual identification of each individual in it.

The process of supporting diversity also impacts the social contacts of students in their classrooms. The diverse environment of each classroom is evidence of the support of districts and teachers to teach the curriculum in education. To see the progress of learners in the art education classes at the schools, we can see that the act works to support art education in the classrooms, and we can also see that a positive change is visible in education. In this research, I have suggested that a professional teacher can easily demonstrate, explain, and teach art education to expand learners' knowledge in the art rooms. This is also about observing, experiencing, learning, and teaching art education in education. Therefore, a professionally qualified teacher can interpret, educate, inform, and explain the terms to support aesthetics, creativity, and artistic mindedness in education. Therefore, art education should be an important part of education at all levels of education to teach the art education curriculum in education. This will help in explaining the basic needs of art education to learners. The individual identity of each individual also supports cultural identity in education. Individual identity is important, valuable, and informal for everyone. Each student can show his or her personal culture, customs, traditions, cultural heritage, and values in the classroom. This must not be able to support racism. The reason revolves around not avoiding teamwork, togetherness, or ignoring peers' values in education. This is true that identities do keep students separate from each other by their cultural values of them. This is also true that students can be checked separately by their personal identities to know and understand the values of each one of them. The issues revolve around separating identities, differences, and racism in education.

# IMPACTS OF RENAISSANCE ART MOVEMENT ON ART EDUCATION

THE PERIOD OF Renaissance was about the rebirth of art to use of the chosen theories for the teachings and learnings through the interpretation, inventiveness, and integration in art education. The works of Masaccio, Alberti, Leonardo, Michelangelo, Raphael, and Vasari had expanded the horizon of the knowledge of the other artists through their chosen theories, methods, materials, themes, and techniques to support their creativity for them. The process of teaching and learning was innovative and helped in understanding the process by not just using the skills to create an artwork at a working place for them.

The process of learning was a chosen path to move on and work on the chosen themes to clarify, implement, apply, and see the results of teachings for them. The use of the knowledge was important instead of the skills for them. During the Renaissance era, the experts had chosen their own theories to teach their learners. They developed their knowledge to incorporate their own ideas for them. They wanted their learners to get ready to work as knowledgeable adults in the future in the Renaissance time. To support the individual identification, they had chosen actions, gestures, body movements, and emotions to support the teachings of the Renaissance era in education. They were willing to spend a huge amount of time on their original artworks and the roles of the academies had also supported the quality of work at that time. They had used the art, literature, and music classes to teach in the learning environment of education at that time. The courses developed the knowledge, skills, and the abilities of the students in education in Europe.

The history has informed that the Renaissance had explained the importance of religious artworks through the chosen themes for the artworks for a long time to complete for an inspiration, spiritual power, and they also used the artworks for the art education. The Renaissance movement's impact on art education has expanded the horizon of knowledge through interpretation, inventiveness, and integration in art education. The process is informative, interesting, valuable, and allows us to use the different lenses by creating and supporting learning through art education. The social, economic, and the financial issues do impact on the quality of the artworks and the process of creation also gets effected by the selection of the materials, teachings in the classes, and the demonstrations for the educational artworks for the teachers in education.

The toxic materials are still not for public schools and the students are also not allowed to inhale these materials in their classes. The collaboration between the teachers and the students can change the social, economic, and cultural levels of the acceptance for them. The Renaissance's impact on art education through integration helped in understanding the combination of the process of making the artworks by using the stories from the religion and era. For example, the details of the developed, detailed, and motivated artworks were sculpted and painted figures with the details about them. The process of teaching was started at the academies in Europe.

They were not offering a proper curriculum for their students, and they were also not using any syllabus for their classes. The thoughts and the ideas were able to support the teachings at that time. The personal thought and the ideologies were called their own theories and those were able to inspire the learners at the academies. The role of the King Louis XIV was incredibly supportive and made the teachings more effective and valuable for the learners in France. The students do need to use the curriculum and support their individual identification.

Studying the impact of the Renaissance movement on visual art education to the present time in Europe through creativity helps to feel, understand, and apply the learning in their own lives. The Renaissance era had given the chances to learn from the experts and Leonardo was a reliable source of information at that time. He used his own thoughts, ideology, and made the decisions to support the teachings in his own way.

The process of description for the learners was successfully developing the quality of the works at that time. They used the knowledge to develop the skills to make the artworks related to the real world and those artworks supported the themes culturally, socially, religiously, and politically at that time. They also supported their individual identification for them. Inventiveness of creativity had an association with learning at that time. The knowledge supported the process of developing the skills for them. They were also able to show their individual identification through their own creativity, aesthetics, and artistic mindedness for them.

To support the integrating process through teachings, the art education teachings were started from the personal theories and the roles of the academies had also supported the teachings of art, literature, and music to the learners without having the curriculum and the syllabus for the students at that time. The process was innovative, engaging, and had a good impact on the learners through the process of learning at the workplaces including workshops and academies in Europe. The impact of the Renaissance on art education explains the importance of religious artworks for inspiration, spiritual power, and innovativeness in art education. The process of teaching gives information about the period of 1450 and conders this time as a modern time and adds the new themes, styles, and theories in it.

This period is a little different than the Carolingian, Romanesque, and Medieval times. The use of the art education teachings has also given evidence for it. Smith supports the use of the curriculum in the modern time, and he also supports the quality of the work of the people in education. The impact of the Renaissance movement on art education was explained through the ideas, plans, teachings, techniques, methods, and the themes without the curriculum in art education. The role of the academies in Italy and France had expanded the knowledge through the teachings of the chosen courses and knowledge was needed more than the skills of work at a workshop. The teachings had improved the skills and developed the knowledge in Europe. Now, the teachers are getting published, and they are also getting more educated through the learning centers and organizations. Art education teachers are expanding the knowledge of learners in education.

# SUSTAINABLE DEVELOPMENT OF METHODS OF TEACHING IN ART EDUCATION

AESTHETICS, KNOWLEDGE, AND collaboration can be used to make creativity, imagination, and artistic mindedness work for the essential parts of sustainable development of methods of teaching in art education. This process can also help to keep the sustainable development more comprehensive, evocative, and operative through the use of literal and practical plannings for an inclusive, engaging, and intrinsic educational environment in it. The process informs about the levels of achievements through the importance of the use of collaboration of the ideas with the process of making the works more meaningful and inspirational to make the works evocative for students in education.

Teachers like to use their literary aesthetics to connect

their thoughts for a practical and literal lesson plan to use to assist their students in the classes. The process of assessment, analyzation, and the use of ideology for the students support the aesthetics for them. The process can make the classroom environment inclusive, engaging, and intrinsic for them. The use of knowledge often helps in explaining the topics' details to students in the classrooms for them. Knowledge reflects through the ideas, plans, themes, and situations that are created through the teaching creativity for this purpose in it.

The collaboration of innovative ideas explains the use of possible ways to make the works more practical, helpful, and consistent for them. Therefore, the use of aesthetics, knowledge, and the collaboration of ideas using the ideas in multiple ways can help in improving the quality of teaching creativity in education. To make the works more engaging, it is important to use the possible ways to support teaching creativity for sustainable development in it. Reviewing the impacts of aesthetics, knowledge, and collaboration on students' lives helps in focusing on the implementations, interpretations, and amplification of these things by using cognitive education strategies in it.

Innovation explores new worlds for students and makes the work more meaningful for them. Teachers cannot build a new person in each student in the classes. Teaching creativity helps in finding the possible ways to use for sustainable development in it. The professionally trained hired teachers, learning abilities of students, and quality of teachings of teachers work effectively in it. If the hired teachers need to complete the training courses, they must be given a chance to develop their teaching methods and skills through a training session to help students for the academics in their classes.

An essential part of teaching revolves around understanding the importance of teaching creativity to support the schools' learnings. To use the curriculum in the classes, the teachers need to develop their own decisions to use the accepted curriculum work in the classes for them. Teaching creativity supports aesthetics and effectiveness of teaching creativity in education. To identify the possible ways to support creativity in teaching for sustainable development in the classrooms, several important lenses can be discussed in it.

The use of the skills for imagination, inventiveness, and visual education helps in learning through the process of completing the assignments for them. Visual literacy also helps in supporting the learning process for the students that can use their own imagination for them. To construct a structure, the discussion is able to support the entire experience is expedient, practical, and essential to me. To support the learnings, students do need to get introduced to each other to own the cultural heritage in the region. They also need to understand the values of the cultures in education. A part of the teaching creativity revolves around cultural awareness and this knowledge supports diversity and inclusion in education. A learning education environment requires the students to concentrate and make the efforts to go higher by working consistently in the classes.

The amplification or extension of the ideas also revolves around aesthetics, knowledge, and collaboration. To use the aesthetic, the teachers do like to support the artistic mindedness of students by supporting the heritage of students of them. Students often get appreciated, acknowledged, and inspired in their classes. The innovation helps engage the teachers with students, parents, and the community. Students do get recognized, conceded, and appreciated in education.

Authenticity supports social justice and diversity in education. The students' cultural impact does affect the students' academic progress each semester in the classrooms. Therefore, they must own the classroom environment to join the class team for their educational activities at the school. The entire process of learning in the learning environment of education impacts their lives. Behavioral issues are also associated with learning in the classrooms. The students' cultural, educational, and collaborative activities support the students learning in their classes. The importance of equity, quality, and inclusion also supports teaching creativity by giving a chance to each student to find a space to represent personal identification in education. The process of teaching is associated with the plans, the implication of the chosen ideas, interpreting the ideas, and applying the chosen ideas for a path to help students in achieving their goals in it and so forth.

# CRITICAL INQUIRY IN THE CURRICULUM IN ART EDUCATION

CRITICAL INQUIRY HELPS in assessing, analyzing, and evaluating the works in education. This process helps in implementing the ideas to accumulate, assemble, and mobilize the moves of them. The curriculum engages students in assignments, activities, learnings, and also helps in achieving the academics by assessing, analyzing, and evaluating their outcomes of them. The curriculum helps in establishing the social and educational contacts of the teachers with students, and the community, and also establishes a good relationship between the teachers-students and student-peers in the classrooms.

Critical inquiry means having an approved curriculum for students and checking the process of implementation by mobilizing the moves for them. This inquiry allows the teachers to make the teaching process more effective, useful, and applicable in the classrooms. The learning process supports the educational activities, constructs the curriculum, and makes the environment innovative for students. This process allows the learners to communicate in their classes to discuss their ideas, plans, and thoughts with each other. Concept interpretation revolves around the use of solid, logical, and empirical evidence to support learning in education. The appropriate selection of the words can make the learning more effective and useful through meaningful, understandable, and analytical works in education.

Conception development revolves around the improvement of learning in education. The appropriate selection of words for improvement, achievement, and more work can help in making the process of learnings more effective in education. Conceptual structure assessment is about building a structure, supporting diversity, and analyzing the details of each part of it. This is about analyzing, assessing, and checking the progress of the learners in education. They often collaborate with their small cadre and use their own knowledge to communicate with each other. The interactions make the classroom environment more inclusive, engaging, and innovative for them.

To support the critical inquiry in the curriculum, the teachers also like to support equality, inclusion, and social learning for them. This situation supports the transnational environment of education. To support the critical inquiry in curriculum, the process of implementation by mobilizing the moves, clarification of the critical learnings through the conceptual theories including the constructivist learning theory and cognitive theory, and the conceptual interpretation supports the developmental process for the structural assessment, critical inquiry, and diversity in education.

Cultural identification helps in supporting the communicational skills in the diverse environment of their classes at school. Inclusion supports the ethnic groups in education. The use of the English language is compulsory in the United States. The learners are required to speak, read, and write in this language and also their communication skills can help in establishing their social contacts to support the educational requirements for the learnings in education. Therefore, critical inquiry needs to support the curriculum by investigating the possibility of using the structural considerations, accentuating, and progression in education.

In the field of education, critical inquiry needs to find the possible ways to use to support the curriculum by investigating the possibility of using the structural considerations, accentuating, and progression in education. In these situations, epistemology supports the real data in education. The facts are related to the real world and critical inquiry can apply but does not work very closely with this term in education. Ontology supports the meanings of the use and application of a theory to see its value and function of it, and this is the opposite of epistemology in education. The ontology may or may not be an important part of the learnings and teachings; this term has value and functions as a valuable term in education, and critical inquiry works effectively for ontology. Constructivist learning theory works closely with Ontology and provides the details of the cultural effects on the learners in education and Cognitive theory is more about memorization in education.

For the constructivist learning theory, the theorist Vygotsky is a reliable source of inspiration and information in education. He supports the process of learning by allowing students to work together to learn more through this process. The use of proper words works better when students get socially engaged, involved, and interact with their peers. A theorist Piaget is a reliable source of inspiration and his information about cognitive theory is popular in education. He supports the learning of everyone's improvement, and this expands their knowledge of them. This has an association with having the ability to understand, memorize, and apply the learnings in education.

The use of the words of the teachers impacts students. Critical Inquiry in the curriculum's common grounds through both theories and the related information can be checked by looking at the details of the similarities and differences in them. For example, the similarities tell us that the learnings help in the improvement of the growth of a learner, learnings about the other cultural aspects impact on students, and the mental growth is important of each learner in memorizing and understanding by sitting in the classes. The differences tell us that each response depends on the chosen moves for Vygotsky and not for Piaget. To support the critical inquiry, the concepts are supposed to be understandable for this purpose and the implications are supposed to be able to make the teachings more effective for it. Analysis allows the educators to analyze, assess, and check the progress of the learnings to make the conceptual works more meaningful, logical, and applicable in education. The curriculum also helps in establishing contacts with students, and the community.

The process of critical inquiry in the curriculum is also related to the learning process of children in the diverse environment of the classes. The majority of the teachers are not bilingual and the learning abilities and understanding of the cultures of the other ethnic students make the teachings more effective for the teachers in education. Epistemology or knowledge supports the real data in education, and ontology or learning supports the value and function of education. Constructivist learning theory works closely with ontology and provides the details of the cultural effects on the learners and cognitive theory is more about memorization in education. In these situations, the critical inquiry is about analyzing, assessing, and checking the progress of the learnings for the assignments, activities, learnings, and practicing in it. Therefore, the use of one language helps in explaining the details to students in the classes.

To support the learning process, the teaching methods are supposed to revolve around inquiries, critical thinking, and critical analysis in education. The teaching strategies are also supposed to be used to make the curriculum more details, instructional, and effective in it. The teachings are also supposed to be consistent, logical, and engaging to keep the classroom environment inclusive for it. The teachers can make the teachings more operative, convenient, and operational for students in education. They can also check the quality of work by using the objectives, classroom rubrics, and related things about it.

The transcultural is important in the classroom environment of education to support the communication skills of each student in and out of the school. Students can also share their own cultural heritage, build a good relationship with the diverse community, and help each other by learning from each other. Learning abilities can help students in making social connections in the classrooms, so they can get introduced to their peers to know more about the cultures, customs, traditions, and values of each other. Therefore, they need to learn about the use of the languages from their teachers for this purpose to make good conversational connections in the classrooms. The teachers are required to teach the curriculum in the English language and the understanding of the cultures of the other ethnic students makes the teachings more effective in education. Therefore, epistemology or knowledge supports the real data in education; ontology or learning supports its value and function of it in the learning environment of education.

The constructivist theory helps in understanding the details of the effects of cultural heritage in education. Cognitive theory is about learning, understanding, and memorizing the details in the classes at school. In the process of learning, the critical inquiry in curriculum supports the assessments for analysis of the academic progress of students in education. The ethnographical designs can support the critical inquiry in curriculum, issues that are impacting the lives of students, and the solutions that can help in making the academic progress of students in education. The impacts talk about two folds in which the solutions can help in understanding the details of them. The first one is about sharing the details of the results that can give the information about the impact of the issues on students and the second one is about checking the details of the impacts to make the changes to support the learning for the academic achievements of students at the school.

A conducted content analysis can help in checking the details of the impact on the educational environment. The process for the methods in the critical inquiry in the curriculum can help in making the process more valuable, ethical, and empirical through a process in education. The implications are noticeable, and they are also able to share the crucial details of the research about the critical inquiry in the curriculum in education. The value of curriculum has informed the students' engagement that makes the evaluations easier for the teachers. The curriculum helps in establishing contacts at the diverse levels of education.

Critical inquiry is able to support the implementation by mobilizing the moves in education. The learning process helps in constructing curriculum, communicational skills, and the concepts of these things in education. Concepts need empirical evidence to support the development, assessment, and building of a structure in it. Critical inquiry makes the process more constructive, supports individual identification, and engages students through pedagogical strategies in it. The values of multiple cultures, nations and their issues are also noticeable in our lives. The curriculum phenomenon also gives a chance to each teacher to use their personal identity, belongings, and the related things in education.

Critical inquiry has helped in understanding the need to support the process by investigating the possible ways to use to make the structural considerations in education. The use of epistemology or knowledge supports facts, and ontology or concept terms have value to share their details of them. The use of constructivist theory supports the effects of the cultural heritage and cognitive theory is about memorizing in the classes at school. Therefore, this research is positively able to share the detail of each part of this entire process to support the critical inquiry in education for it.

# MULTICULTURALISM IN URBAN ART EDUCATION

MULTICULTURALISM HAS INFORMED us about the importance of critical race theory, critical multiculturalism, and social justice that are associated with multiculturalism in art education. The experiences, practices, observations, interpretations, learnings, and awareness of students are important in education. Instructional practices help in understanding the details of the importance of critical multiculturalism in it. This information informs that the racial inequalities, the diverse educational atmosphere of education, and the importance of social justice make the process work for it. The use of multiple ways to discuss the important parts of art education, social justice, and multiculturalism have explained several things in it, and critical race theory is included in it.

Critical race theory supports ethnic groups of students by protecting the rights of each individual in education.

The impacts of critical race theory on urban art education and urban learnings inform us about the importance of each ethnic student in the larger cities, the overcrowded classrooms, fewer chances to ask questions in each class, and also fewer chances to get the attention of teachers in each class. This information has informed us that racism and the differences between the communities are also not supposed to be able to harm the learning of learners in education. This information also informs that race is an identity and informs about the personal identification of each ethnic student and racism is about just supporting own ethnic community and rejecting the importance and cultural values of the other communities in education. This information has also informed that each ethnic student is different, unique, and essential for the teachers. Therefore, they need to learn about the cultural values of each other by ignoring the difference between them.

For observations and interpretations, the inspirations, arguments, and interpretations of multiculturalism are important in education. Multiculturalism supported each individual's personal identity, diversity as a whole, and self-awareness to support learners against abstraction in education. Abstraction has no concern with any cultural identification. There are no rules and regulations that can support multiculturalism through abstraction except for having the creativity to make modern and contemporary art that cannot inform, educate, and show the cultural identity of any community in it.

Identities of the communities, social norms, and culturally responsive teachings impact the country's educational atmosphere. Therefore, multiculturalism is also about diversity, cultural heritage, and traditions in education. This information is able to support the basic concept of multiculturalism in education. As a civilized person of a civilized society, I am required to know and understand the values and importance of other cultures to perform my civic duty as well.

Multiculturalism can inform us about the importance of customs, cultures, traditions, values, and the cultural heritage of students in schools. This is able to give a chance to support each student's individual identity in the classes. This is not supposed to be able to support racism. This is supposed to be used to see the personal identity of each student to get introduced to them. This process is able to make the difference between having a personal identity and adopting the culture of the United States as a resident and a citizen of the United States. This process has engaged the students to make the classroom environment engaging, and innovative for them. They do represent their personal religious beliefs, racial identifications, and their native languages in education. This process is getting combined by adopting the American cultural heritage for them. The process of having a personal identification, adopting the

American culture, and combing both cultures to become a part of education as a successful person is useful, effective, and accepted in education. Therefore, multiculturalism as a way of information is supposed to be accepted, adopted, and evaluated by hired professionally trained teachers.

The educational materials in the classrooms make the process work for students in the schools. These plans, programs, and evaluations can help the diverse students at the schools in education as well. Another important part of the teachings and learnings revolves around self-hesitancy, self-utterance, and self-knowledge in urban art education. This is able to give a chance to each student to represent his or her own individual identity in the classes. This is not supposed to be able to support racism. This is supposed to be used to see the personal identity of each student to get introduced to them. This process is also supposed to be able to make the differences between having a personal identity and adopting the culture of the United States as a resident and a citizen of the United States. They do represent their personal religious beliefs, racial identifications, and their native languages in education. This process is getting combined by adopting the American cultural heritage with their own cultures for them. The process of having a personal identification, adopting the American culture, and combing both cultures to become a part of education as a successful person is useful, effective, and accepted in education.

Therefore, multiculturalism as a way of information is supposed to be getting accepted, adopted, and evaluated by hiring professionally trained teachers, purchasing, and providing special educational materials in the classrooms to make the process work for students in the schools. These plannings, programs, and evaluations can help the diverse students at the schools in education as well.

Urban education revolves around equity, equality, and inclusion in education. Equity supports impartiality, justice, and fairness in it. Equality supports equivalence, likeness, and parity. Inclusion revolves around insertion, presence, and enclosure in education. This information supports the diverse environment of education by informing about the equal rights and responsibilities of students in education. Therefore, teachers are willing to work with students to keep the environment inclusive, engaging, and innovative in education. The process of interpretation, collaboration, amplification, and also the use of interpersonal strategies work to support multiculturalism in urban art education.

Critical race theory has supported ethnic groups of students by protecting the rights of each individual in education. The research has informed that the importance of art education can be seen through the research, and it is hard to discuss the impacts of critical race theory researchers in education. Diversity and urban learning can inform about the importance and understanding of it. This information has informed us that multiculturalism has an association with critical race theory in art education. These learnings must not be able to support racism and differences between the communities, and they are also not supposed to be able to have an adverse impact on the learnings of learners in education.

Critical multiculturalism in urban art education has the ability to support equity, equality, and inclusion in the diverse environment of education. This information has informed us that the educational policy of the system has always supported students without keeping them separate by the individual identity of each student in education. The process of support always keeps students involved and engaged, and the classroom environment also gets innovative as well.

In this situation, social justice is able to support the individuality of each community, civil society, and comprehensive environment in education. A comprehensive environment is supposed to be essential, inspirational, and innovative in education. Civil society is more about constructing, considering, and collaborating with the members of the civil society. The community has a role to perform civic duties and social contacts with others. All of these important parts of education are associated with multiculturalism in education. The involvement of students, individual identity, and not understanding the importance of the values of other ethnic groups are causing problems in the classes. Another critical issue revolves around the need to use a correct curriculum for art education classes to support learning in the classrooms. Each student's personal involvement shows the personal learnings, and personal abilities to understand the basic concepts of multiculturalism and also helps each student in finding a way for each individual to show his or her personal learnings, knowledge, and skills in education.

The process of individual identification has three bad impacts, including supporting racism, showing the individuality that can be different than others, and not accepting the power of others. Therefore, it is important to support individual identification of each learner for individuality by rejecting differences to stay united at the school. The purpose of this research is to investigate the impacts of multiculturalism on critical race theory, critical multiculturalism, and social justice on urban art education by finding ways to make a good impact on students for a better future in education. The research is not highlighting differences and accepting individuality as a source of identification in education.

Individuality supports the individual identification of each individual by informing about the cultures, customs, traditions, values, and cultural heritage of each student in it. Teachers do like to use their different methods of teaching to educate, inform, and support their learners in their classes from K-12. In colleges and universities, the process of supporting students exceeds the limits and provides more guidance, help, and approves educational materials to keep the classroom environment more inclusive, engaging, and innovative for them. The learnings do need more support for learners in it. This informs the use of more educational materials that are available for students to use in their classes. One of the possibilities revolves around the use of OER in education. These sources do support each individual's personal identification and also provide free educational materials so they can collaborate, cooperative, and communicate with each other.

Diversity is the beauty of the country. The entire country is full of the people of the world. They represent their customs, cultures, traditions, values, and cultural heritage through their own art, dance, food, music, sport, and clothing. Each individual is an ambassador of his or her own background. This information also helps to know and understand the importance of languages by lining style and developing interests in education. As an American, I do like to support the diverse culture of the country. I also like to educate, inform, and support the educational needs of students in the classrooms. As a student and educator, I do work to support collaboration, implementation, interpretation, and amplification of these things in education.

When we support diversity, we support the educational, social, cultural, and political norms in education. Therefore, social norms, social justice, and social involvement are needed in education. Social justice is an important part of education. This process is able to support the individual identification of each individual in the educational environment, comprehensive environment, and inductive environment of the country. An educational environment helps in making the process of learning work by providing a space for each individual to work, learn, and use the learnings to have influence at certain levels of education. A comprehensive environment is essentially able to support, inspire, and inform each learner in the classes. This valuable information informs that an inductive environment is able to indicate, inform, educate, and guide the right path so the learners can move forward to achieve their goals in their lives. This information informs that the process of learning is associated with collaboration, consideration, and communication to make the learnings work in education. This also supports the involvement of cultural heritage, individuality, and identity of each individual in it.

All of the important parts of art education can help in making the good process of conducting the research, collecting the data, and the findings are also helpful in education. The impacts, ways to support learners, and the process of keeping the work consistent, logical, and ethical are important in education. This information also can support the work for multiculturalism to make cultural pluralism work for the diverse community of education.

The diverse culture of the diverse community of the country supports individual identity and unity of the country. In the process of supporting the educational atmosphere of the country, we do need to support and promote the efforts to keep the critical multicultural education work in the system. critical race theory is also an important part of it. Therefore, critical race theory is not about the development of ideas, practices, and theories in the classes. Critical race theory is also about having an analytical approach to get involved by supporting the social norms in education. Multiculturalism's impacts are checked to inform, educate, and support students' identification, not to keep the identities of students away from their peers in the classrooms.

The classroom environment is discussed to keep the environment inclusive, engaging, and innovative in urban institutions. This is an important part of the learning process to use the observations, experiences, and knowledge in the classes. This can support urban learning in urban education. This process also informs about the details of the methods, themes, and ideas that are reflected through the research in it. The investigation process revolves around assortment, impartiality, and insertion in education. The process also highlights the important parts of teaching to keep the entire work transparent in education. This information is used to investigate the various parts of the cultural, social, and gender norms' influence through the semi-structured interviews in it.

The components of qualitative research design including the abstract, purpose of study, literature review, methods, and findings are needed in the process of conducting the research in it. The problems are explored, use of qualitative methods to develop theories, not the reasons, emergent processes, ethics, and issues are addressed by informing about them. The purpose statement is about the importance of selecting a topic and discussions in it. The importance of validations and evaluations, including validity, central imagination, reliability, and eleven inquiries, are needed in the research process.

The trustworthiness, applicability, consistency, neutrality, internal validity (depending on variables), external validity, reliability, and reliability that depended on consistency, dependability, predictability, and transferability can be discussed in it. Overlap methods help in understanding the details of one way of conducting arguments, stepwise replications, and confirmability in it. Politics of evidence, criteriology about the different criteria, member check key, and the use of triangulation is in it. Trustworthiness refers to the systematic rigor of the chosen research study design, the credibility of the conducted research, and the applicability of the research methods to see the effectiveness of each part of the process in education. Interviews support a couple of things all the time, and this information revolves around using a focus group, and also a face-to-face interview for this purpose.

Inconsistency, overlapping methods, and stepwise replication inform that the chosen methods of carrying arguments need attention in it. Body language observations are noticeable for an interviewer to know and understand the behavior of an interviewee in this process. Semi-structured data collection can support the method of qualitative research. Credibility refers to the trust in the collected data, and the responses of the participants also support the research in it. The consistency of the collected data helps in understanding the use of criteria, including dependability (overlapping method, triangulation, reliability, examining the process of data collection, how the data was kept, and accuracy of data) in it.

Confirmability helps to support confirmability audit, objectivity to examine the product to confirm that the findings of interpretations and the chosen recommendations are getting supported by the collected data that helps in understanding the details of the data that are showing the responses of the participants, and the researcher's personal biases are not getting included in it. Transferability helped in understanding its effectiveness, including the thick descriptions by discussing its use in multiple settings and external validity in the research. Authenticity supports the process of observing the personal emotions and behavioral gestures of participants to make the process of observation work in an essential manner.

The extensions of trustworthiness expanded the knowledge about prolonged engagement, persistent observations, and triangulation (sources, methods, and investigations). The extension of the topic revolved around the philosophical assumptions, research approach, the role of the researcher, data collection, data analysis, validity of findings (member checking), and ethical issues (anonymity, conflict of interest, inconsistency, and data collection). The details about the ethical issues, sources, forms, array, and activities informed the quality of the research. Purposeful sampling strategy, maximum variation sampling, sample size, forms of data, interview protocol, the procedure for preparing, and conducting interviews, observational protocol, and design and application of them. Context is about transferability, semi-structured conducted research and collected data, the role of participants, and the roles of a researcher in it.

Data collection, transcript, responses of participants, the process of collecting the data, and research design in it. IRB design's details and format, including a concert form, standard, ethics, and safety of participants, are included in it. Face-to-face interviews are required for qualitative research in education. This part of the research gives multiple options for the researchers including interviewing a small cadre of interviewees for the face-to-face interviews, individual interviews, and having large group of the interviewees for the qualitative research in education. Another viable way to complete this part of the research revolves around a telephonic interview to cover the distances from one location to another location for this purpose and so forth.

# PHILOSOPHY OF TEACHING AND LEARNING ART EDUCATION IN THE 21ST CENTURY

THE PHILOSOPHY OF teaching and learning art education in the 21st century revolves around philosophical thinking, assessment, and the complexity theory to compare the works in the 21st century. The philosophy of teaching and learning in the 21st century tells us about writing, reading, and thinking philosophically by observing, assessing, analyzing, evaluating, and checking the results of them. Writing has an association with the several things including introducing a topic in the beginning, thinking, and talking about own beliefs. The reason behind this decision also tells us the details of mental and physical growth and an external environmental influence on people. It is a part of the learning process of the philosophy of teaching.

An explanation of the chosen topics can make the work more valuable in the classes. An examination of the gathered information can give a chance to review the work. When the students evaluate their work, they can understand the importance of the use of the sources for them. In the field of art education, this situation revolves around the use of creativity, aesthetics, and artistic mindedness in it. This process also supports visual literacy, visual learning, critical thinking, object-based learning, and project-based learning in it. Critical thinking supports visual development, the function of art, and the public space in it.

Critical thinking's association with visual development informs us about the importance of the shape, form, depth, and colors of artwork in art education. The spectrum can be broader, lengthy, informal, or formal to make the process work in it. Another important part of this research informs that urban art education can be taken as a source of information, inspiration, and a form of discipline to expand the knowledge of learners in education.

The teachers are required to lead their students to improve the process of learning in the learning environment of education. They do want to let their students grow mentally, physically, and spiritually. The students are supposed to be able to use their prior knowledge and creativity to survive in their classes. They are also supposed to be able to learn and memorize things in their lives because their learning abilities will have an impact not only on their lives; they will also have an impact on the lives of others. The process must be consistent, and the learners are supposed to be willing to learn from their teachers. The life of Socrates is a good example of it because he was willing to brighten the lives of the youth of Athens by teaching about the philosophy of life in his time, which gave a popularity to him. No written evidence was available about his work for the youth. The only source of information was Plato who was willing to store, save, and memorize his sayings for the people of Athens.

In one of the famous paintings about the death of Socrates, Socrates is surrounded by his friends and Plato is also with him. Socrates is about to drink a bowl full of Hemlock which is a slow poison. His own wife is a part of this subject matter, and she is standing at a distance and looking at him. Plato looks incredibly old in this picture. He is supposed to look young because he was not older than Socrates. All of the facial features and face expressions are telling their viewers that they are with the great scholar of Athens. Therefore, Plato saved all of the things about Socrates and shared with others. Plato was a reliable source of information in the world of philosophy. Several artworks were made on him.

We just have to try to understand the details of them.

The reason behind this decision is amazingly simple. The teachers want their students to work on their assignments by doing research to dig for the details of their chosen topic to complete the work. The entire process is incredibly challenging for them. They have to select a topic to work on it. They need to get approval from their teachers to make their work an officially approved one. They need to use appropriate sources from their chosen media for their work. They have to go through the entire process of learning to complete the task and to meet the higher standards of education in the classrooms. The results or the outcomes can give a better picture of the entire efforts of the students to their teachers. The teachers have the authority to accept and apricate the efforts of the students to encourage them in their classes. The main purpose is to let them grow mentally and physically by giving them a chance to work on their projects or their assignments in the classrooms.

The teachers do want to focus on learning in schools. The main reason is the mental growth of their students because they want their students to get ready for their higher classes by getting ready for their AP or college level classes in their classrooms. Philosophical thinking is about thinking philosophically by respecting the views of other people. A knowledgeable person's kindness, broad-mindedness, and truthfulness can bring a positive change in the learning environment of an institution. The process of thinking philosophically gives a chance to research by thinking philosophically. It has to go through several stages to get to the destination by doing the analyzation, assessment, interpretation, evaluation, and checking the outcomes of it. Complexity theory is about the philosophy of teaching and learning by reading, writing, and doing research to know more about it. The process of doing research opens up several things for the researcher and gives a chance to expand the knowledge of the researcher itself and also as well as the readers through this process. Philosophy shares different theories about the possible ways of using the philosophy of teaching from different perspectives. I agree with it because teaching is a challenging job, and it is a big commitment for the teachers.

The classroom management, time-management, and the policies and procedures of the artrooms are important for learners. They use their time wisely by explaining the nature of each assignment in the beginning, demonstrating, and walking around to check and answer the questions of their students. They teach their various levels every day. They do not avoid, insult, or harass their students. The environment of the classes is friendly and free of all kinds of pressures. They are willing to provide art supplies and sometime, the art students do want to order their own supplies to complete their work in their classes by getting help from their teachers. They share ideas with each other.

They are allowed to help their classmates by exchanging their themes, methods, and materials with each other.

The art-teachers are using various sources from the different medias to teach in their art rooms because; they want to expand the horizon of the knowledge of their students in the learning environment of the art rooms. the philosophy of teaching and learning in the 21st century gives a chance to know about philosophical thinking, learning to do an assessment, and the complexity theory to compare the works in the 21st century.

The students can observe, assess, analyze, evaluate, and check the results of their own work and as well as the works of their classmates in the classrooms. Learning theories including behaviorism, cognitivism, constructivism, teaching principles including active learning, problem-based learning, cooperative learning, and scholarly teaching including clear goals, adequate preparation, appropriate methods, meaningful results, effective presentation, and reflective critique can give a better picture of it. We can use the words of integrative learning, mental and physical growth, and the roles of the teachers can be compared with the roles of the doctors. We can say that the process of learning is more about taking it as a logic, instrumental, talking about formation, taking the field of teaching same as instruction in the institutions, and the use of the authority in our lives. This process can be controllable, universal, linear, and stable in complexity theory.

# INNOVATION BY USING TECH IN ART EDUCATION

TECH EDUCATION HAS informed and explained several parts of the use and importance of tech tools in education. I have used several tech tools for doctoral work, and each one has expanded the horizon of my knowledge in multiple ways and has also given me a chance to learn more about the different techniques, methods, and use of them. Face-to-face and online teachings and learnings are important in education. They keep students engaged, involved, and connected in them. The modern tech tools have informed me about the use, understanding to see the importance of the collected data, the analysis of data, the learnings of students, the understanding of students, the impact of instructional teaching, and application of the teaching methods in them.

The whole entire process has helped in making the work more consistent, ethical, and meaningful in it. The use of tech tools in supporting online teaching and learning by using online sources supports personal thoughts, use of modern processes of teaching and learning, graphs, analysis, the percentage of the collected data, the analysis of data, the learnings of students, understanding of students, and a good impact of instructional teaching to make the works look more accurate, functional, and detailed in it.

Mind Mapping is popular in the United States. This process informs us that we can make any colorful, detailed, and useful Mind Maps for any use in education. This process has expanded my knowledge through the practice and use of innovative ideas by engaging, informing, and helping in making the works more useful in a modern way. the use of tech tools for curriculum, lesson plans, and educational activities for learners are supportive in education. We can revise, learn, and understand more about the importance of the educational environment of the classes to keep the environment innovative, engaging, and inclusive in education. Modern school report card at the state level and also at the local district level are useful, effective, and important by finding essential information about a district, checking the educational ranking, and informing about the details of the academic achievements of students in them. The public record is accessible, and reliable, and provides information about schools and districts of the entire country. It is easy to gather the research by selecting the different elements, editing the design, selecting the relevant images, changing the fonts, and colors, and keeping the alignment together for it. Screencasting has informed about the use of dialogue delivery, body movement, use of facial expression, and the impacts of togetherness. Team leadership, community engagement, emotional involvement, and communications skills do get developed through collaboration in it. This entire process is informative, interesting, and valuable, and has informed us about the importance of individuality, individual identification, and personal belonging to us.

The entire Department of Education supports diversity, ethnic students' personal identity, cultural heritage, personal development, personal learning, and personal belonging in it. This process requires copyright images, valid information, peer reviewed articles through the different databases, and related details in it. The use of an introductory video, the process of learning, instructional resources to peers for relevant artifact creativity, and to share on social media are always supportive educators as well as learners. Our efforts have given us a chance to inform, instruct, and provide the readings, instructions, and relevant information to them. We have also shared our ideas, plans, questions, and related research for this purpose. Our collaboration, facilitation, and instructions are highly appreciated by our peers.

The use of mobile apps and smart devices helps in

keeping personal observations, experiences, teachings, and learnings in an order in education. The use of advantages and disadvantages of OER helps in checking the details of teachings and learnings of administrators, researchers, professors, and learners that are using these reliable resources free of charge for them. Tech tools are giving a new perspective to make the learnings work in it. The use and effectiveness of norms in face-to-face, hybrid, and online learning are also important in education. Teachers do like to use norms to make the teachings work for them. It is important to know and understand the essential information about them.

In higher education, they help in selecting the correct design, adding the elements, and changing the color scheme to make the artifacts look more logical and meaningful for us. All of these learnings are useful, and effective, and will last forever in education. The process of learning is advanced, collaborative, expressive, innovative, instructional, and supportive in education. The process of learning revolves around tech tools, including Canva, Google Forms, MindMeister, Poll Everywhere, PowerPoint, Screencast-O-Matic, Voki, and YouTube in education. The instructional, informational, cultural, and educational environment supports the process of revising, learning, and understanding the importance of the educational environment of the classes to keep the environment innovative, engaging, and inclusive in education. They also help in gathering the educational information, selecting the different elements, editing the design, selecting the relevant images, changing the fonts, and colors, and keeping the alignment together to make the artifacts more useful in it. They also support learnings, observations, inspirations, and experiences in education as well.

# SOCIAL JUSTICE ART EDUCATION THROUGH BLOOM'S TAXONOMY IN MEDIA LITERACY IN URBAN EDUCATION

## Introduction

THE IMPORTANCE OF social justice art education through Bloom's Taxonomy in media literacy helps to integrate the essential works through self-awareness, social dimensions, and urban art education. To interpret, assess, analyze, and evaluate the quality of the artworks of ethnic students in education, social justice allows the ethnic students to create their artworks by working independently to explore the new world for them. They can use their own creativity, knowledge, skills, and abilities in their classrooms. Therefore, art educators do not give preferences to students by gender, race, color, and ethnicity in education.

Self-awareness gives a chance to share personal choices and preferences through the creativity and the aesthetics of the art in the classrooms.

The art teachers also provide instructions and allow students to use their creativity. Self-confidence makes students feel better, more knowledgeable, and more skillful in education. The social dimensions are about the social interactions, social practice, and social interfaces in social justice art education. Social justice is a way to use thoughts, ideas, and techniques to make the artworks as an individual for self-expression. Art education is a process of teaching the importance of art, education, and art education to students in education. The art teachers do want students to use their own prior knowledge to share their creativity with others. Therefore, the process of making the artwork expands the knowledge through the process of making the artworks by themselves. Social justice also allows ethnic students to create their artwork by working independently in their classes. They do have to use their ideas, techniques, methods, and materials to make the artworks to show their contextual skills in education.

The process of learning plays an important part in the lives of students and supports the process of implementation, interpretation, collaboration, amplification, and applications that can impact the use of interpersonal, intrapersonal, and cognitive strategies to support the progress of each one of them. When students want to understand the educational needs at the school to find the answers to their questions, concentrate in their classes, and get well-trained teachers in their classes, they try to find trained teachers. Students are also the first priority for the teachers in education. Therefore, they are supposed to be able to develop their knowledge, skills, and abilities in education, and they are also supposed to be able to make their own decisions by themselves. Bloom's taxonomy shares the classification by dividing the taxonomy into six sections.

This taxonomy explains the importance of understanding, conception, function, assessment, production, and consideration to see the outcomes of these things in social justice art education. The art students can use taxonomy to learn more by using the possible ways to get checked by themselves. Art educators can also check students by using taxonomy in education. They can use the taxonomy for art education to set the standards for art education students in education. The provided art education with Bloom's taxonomy can help achieve their goals, and they will also use the provided guideline to move on to better academics for them. The higher level of thinking can also get support from the art education teachers. They can use their own creativity, ideas, and aesthetic sense for their creation. The use of Bloom's taxonomy also supports the idea of using action words for students in the curriculum. This information supports the use of Bloom's taxonomy in education.

The classification of Bloom's taxonomy has informed that each section revolves around a certain part of the learning and must be taken care of by educators in education. The use of digital literacies in social justice art education informs about the importance of learning to expand the horizon of knowledge in education. This also informs about having the understanding to assess, analyze, check, explain, and get evaluated in education. Learnings impact learners in multiple ways. They do like to use their observations, learnings, experiences, inspirations, and knowledge in their classes. It is important to know and understand the use and effectiveness of individual identity in social justice art education through Bloom's taxonomy in media literacy, the impact of cultural heritage on the urban educational environment and highlights the differences in cultural heritage in education. Media literacy and the use of media through visual literacy, visual learning, and visual awareness are discussed in it.

Art educators like to expand the knowledge of students without supporting the ethnicity of students in education and the process can be supported through the use of Bloom's taxonomy to explain the importance of understanding, conception, function, assessment, production, and consideration to see the outcomes of them social justice art education. The entire process of teaching and learning must be consistent, ethical, and meaningful and the educational environment of classrooms also must be inclusive, engaging, and innovative for them. Urban classrooms have a diverse environment in the larger cities of the United States. This information also informs about the importance of equity, equality, and inclusion in the diverse environment of the country and students do have equal rights, advantages, and privileges for them.

## Self-awareness

Self-awareness gives a chance to share personal choices and preferences through the creativity and the aesthetics of the art in the classrooms by supporting self-confidence, social interface, and social practice in it. The art teachers also provide instructions and allow students to use their creativity. Social justice is a way to use thoughts, ideas, and techniques to make the artworks as an individual for self-expression. Art education is a process of teaching the importance of art, education, and art education to students in education. This information is an integral part of the research and the art teachers do want students to use their own prior knowledge to share their creativity with others. Therefore, the process of making the artwork expands the knowledge through the process of making the artworks by themselves and art educators do not want to give preferences to students by gender, race, color, and ethnicity in education.

Social change also has an association with social justice art education which supports self-confidence, self-expression, and self-awareness in education. Social change also allows art students to develop their knowledge through the process of learning in the learning environment of education by doing the work, completing the process, and making the artworks to share their talent by themselves. Civic literacy supports the self-awareness, self-confidence, and self-expression of students and this process allows students to find their own space through social justice art education. The use of time, energy, and effort can improve the quality of the artworks of students in the classrooms. The knowledge of the philosophy of art education supports the process of using theory and practice to improve the quality of the works for them. Therefore, students do need moral support from their teachers and their classmates to get accepted and social justice art education helps build confidence and awareness by supporting their literacy levels in education. The higher level of education allows the teachers to use their knowledge, skills, and abilities for their students to teach in their classes. The critical analysis also allows the teachers to check the quality of the artworks by assessing the artworks critically to them. The outcomes also support the process of learning in education as well.

Self-confidence helps students in multiple ways. They feel more educated, self-determined, and they also can support their own plans by themselves. To improve their knowledge, skills, and abilities, they do have to move on for a better and brighter future for themselves. The teachers also have to interpret, amplify, elaborate, and evaluate by letting students collaborate their own ideas with the process of making the artwork by themselves. This social-emotional learning helps in growing with creativity and enthusiasm. The participation of students in art education does support self-confidence by letting students establish their social contacts with others, and civic engagement, involvement, and a sense of responsibility also support their civic duty , and also allows to show interest in these things at their school. They also like to be engaged, involved, and connected to learn and create more for them.

Sometimes, students do not have any access to the art classrooms, and they do not know how to explore new worlds for them. There is a whole lot more to learn for them, and their self-confidence can develop their thinking skills and make students think about the possible ways to use to make the artworks without having the proper education, knowledge, skills, methods, materials, and peers in their lives. When they create something without getting any guidance from educated people and peers, they do not learn much through the process of making the artworks, because they have limited knowledge, skills, and awareness of the process of making the artworks for them, and the teachers, the use of pedagogy can also help in understanding the process of learning the theory and practicing it in multiple ways. To achieve these goals, students need to stay connected, engaged, and motivated in education, and they also need to explore new worlds to learn more from their teachers, and the teachers need to get trained to improve the quality of the teaching for better teaching at school.

## Social dimensions

Social dimensions revolve around social identification, social interactions, and social norms, and social justice gives students a chance to share their influences through their artworks by themselves. Diversity supports the customs, cultures, traditions, values, and languages in social justice art education. As an individual, a student artist can produce themes to represent personal identity, individuality, and interactions with the community to support identity in the community. Community-based involvement and community-based learning supports the process of mental growth in multiple ways. We can enhance social involvement in social justice art education to have a good impact on others and also to convey a message to others, students need to make meaningful artworks in the classrooms. The interactions and the progress of making artworks will let students use their own ideas to find a space to share and explain the basic themes of their artwork to others.

Social justice art education helps students understand their own personalities through their own choices and their preferences for them. Art teachers do like to help students by giving them chances to use their instruction and allowing students to use their creativity, choices, and preference for them. This learning process gives a chance to know about the personal choices, preferences, and abilities in making decisions in the lives of students in education. Students need to get their public space in education to talk about social justice in art education and share their knowledge, skills, and abilities with others. In education, the public space gives a chance to learn through the process of learning in the learning environment of education.

Social justice art education helps students understand their own personalities through their own choices and their preferences for them. Art teachers do like to help students by giving them chances to use their instruction and allowing students to use their creativity, choices, and preference for them. This learning process gives a chance to know about the personal choices, preferences, and abilities in making decisions in the lives of students in education. Students need to get their public space in education to talk about social justice in art education and share their knowledge, skills, and abilities with others. In education, the public space gives a chance to learn through the process of learning in the learning environment of education.

Self-awareness supports the qualities of the art students by supporting their social and moral ethics in their lives. Students do learn multiple things by collaborating with fellow artists, and their teamwork can also support their team leader in multiple ways. Self-awareness has an association with self-expression that can give a chance to explore new worlds by improving the knowledge, skills, and abilities in education. Social justice in art education supports learners in expanding their knowledge by letting students work with others and this process has a big spectrum and moves in different directions for students at various levels. Students can take advantage of it by competing with the other students at their own school and the other schools in education.

The importance of social justice art education can also be seen through the development of art education in education. Therefore, diversity supports on an equal basis, and students can find a space to work for them; diversity represents the customs, cultures, traditions, values, and languages in the social justice art education. Social identification is about the use of different methods of teaching to make the teachings work for each individual, each individual owns his or her identity shares personal cultural heritage as a personal identification. Students are different from each other, and their cultures, customs, traditions, values, religions, and cultural heritage are supporting the identities of them. This impact must not keep students away from each other, and the importance of lived experiences, observations, learnings of learners is important in education, and by using the essential parts of lived experiences, learners can make the process work for them.

## Urban art education

Social justice art education through Bloom's Taxonomy in media literacy informs about the importance of the urban environment of art education. This information is also associated with equity, equality, and inclusion. Equity is able to support justice to make the process of learning work in the learning environment of education. Equality is able to support the similarities between students in it. Inclusion is about placing students in the urban educational environment of education. Diversity of education impacts on the social contacts of learners in the classrooms. The process or teaching is impacting on the impacts of learners and letting students incorporate the observations, learnings, experiences, and inspirations in their own ways. Therefore, social justice art education through Bloom's Taxonomy in media literacy in the urban environment of education helps students understand their educational needs at the school by finding the solutions to their social, educational, personal, political, economic, and educational needs education.

Media literacy is able to expand the knowledge of learners in multiple ways in urban art education. Multicultural students do face several problems for several reasons in urban education, and they have to adapt to the culture of the other ethnic students by communicating with them. Language barriers also affect communicational skills, and this issue does not let the students establish their social, cultural, and educational contacts with the other students in urban education. The process or teaching is impacting on the impacts of learners and letting students incorporate the observations, learnings, experiences, and inspirations in their own ways. Therefore, social justice art education through Bloom's Taxonomy in media literacy in the urban environment of education helps students understand their educational needs at the school by finding the solutions to their social, educational, personal, political, economic, and educational needs education. Media literacy is able to expand the knowledge of learners in multiple ways in urban art education. Multicultural students do face several problems for several reasons in urban education, and they have to adapt to the culture of the other ethnic students by communicating with them. Language barriers also affect communicational skills, and this issue does not let the students establish their social, cultural, and educational contacts with the other students in urban education.

The teachers do take the responsibility to support the students by helping in the classrooms with their assignments, research, and other educational activities of them. The teachers do not give preferences to their students by ethnicity. The use of resources, including technology, school supplies, internet, and the electronic devices helps in conducting research, saving the works, and presenting the research in education. Using different browsers, devices, programming, and websites expands the students' knowledge every day. Lacking resources' impact on the academics of the students and financial funding are some of the big reasons behind them, and the lack of federal, state, and local funding cannot support the learning process in urban education. The lack of trained teachers affects the progress of the students in education. Therefore, to teach students in urban settings, trained and knowledgeable teachers are needed in the classrooms for students to expand their knowledge of them, and the behavior of students affects the values of the living society that requires unity and integrity from them.

The teachers understand that students must complete the assignments, core curriculum, theory, and practice for the students in a timely manner; they do not need to ignore the importance of their social values in education. The process of interpretation supports the implementation of the ideas by finding ways to improve the quality of the works in the system, and students need to incorporate the teaching methods in the learning environment of education. This information informs that the teachers must improve the quality of the education, curriculum, and inclusive and engaging classroom environment, and inclusion to educate the ethnic students in the classrooms. Interpersonal, intrapersonal, and cognitive strategies do have good impacts on them. For civil society's civic duties, students need to construct, consider, and collaborate to work together, and teachers must improve the educational quality to keep the classroom environment more inclusive and engaging for them.

## Discussion

This research has informed about the use and effectiveness of individual identity in social justice art education through Bloom's taxonomy in media literacy, the impact of cultural heritage on the urban educational environment, and the differences in education. Media literacy works effectively in education, and the use of media through visual literacy, visual learning, and visual awareness also works in it. Self-awareness, social dimensions, and the urban art educational environment support social justice art education in media literacy, and Bloom's taxonomy has explained the importance of understanding, conception, function, assessment, production, and consideration in it. Urban classrooms have a diverse environment in the United States; therefore, the urban educational environment supports equity, equality, and inclusion in the country. Students have the advantages, honors, and privileges in their classes, and they also have access to the use of the media to learn each day. Professionally trained educators are in education, and they use their teaching methods each day to educate their learners through the methods of teaching media in the classrooms. The entire process of teaching and learning works each day in education as well.

# SOCIAL CONSTRUCTIVIST ART EDUCATION IN AN URBAN EDUCATIONAL ENVIRONMENT OF EDUCATION

Social constructivist art education is an important part of cultural representation, cultural awareness, and cultural productivity to support each ethnic student in a sociocultural environment of education. The process of teaching can support learners by supporting the social norms, social awareness, and social production in it. The process of constructivist art education has informed about the importance of it through one of the famous philosophers called, Vygotsky. The process of learning is associated with the use of creativity, aesthetics, and artistic mindedness. Collaboration supports cooperation, understanding, and also entirety. Constructivism also informs about personal learning, personal experiences, and personal knowledge through Piaget for it. This also informs that social constructivism is about social norms, social awareness, and social production, and this is different than constructivism.

Social constructivist art education supports social, cultural, and personal contacts to know the importance of other cultures. My personal knowledge, observations, and learnings have informed me about it. He has supported Vygotsky's collaborative works make the process of learning work for learners in it. Collaborative work helps in sharing personal ideas, plans, and thinking with peers to each individual, and no individual gets a preference for it. Ethnicity is able to inform about the customs, cultures, traditions, values, and cultural heritage of each ethnic student in education. Individual identification also helps in understanding the details of the cultural heritage of students. Individual identification is not supposed to be able to support racism in it. This process can help to support each student's work so they can make their work more meaningful, ethical, and useful in it. The process of implementation, interpretation, collaboration, and amplification is also supposed to be consistent in it.

My personal knowledge also has informed me that Piaget has informed about social constructivist art education by sharing his own ideas, plans, and suggestions to make the process of teaching and learning work for each individual in it. Students learn from their own experiences, observations, and planning. They can show their learning by communicating and socializing with peers, and Piaget's constructivism supports personal learning, personal knowledge, and also personal awareness in it. The learning process can support the realization, clarification, intensification, collaboration, and real-world inspiration to extend the process in it. The values of subjective experiences, creativity, and aesthetics have informed the works of Dewey in education.

From my perspective, constructivism has informed the perception to support realization and observational works by having the understanding to make the process of teaching and learning work in it. Constructivism also has informed about the consciousness to support realization, perception, and awareness in it. The process provides opportunities for educators and students to establish social and cultural contacts with others. This can help in sharing the details of lived experiences and communal contacts in it. In the process of learning about the importance of social constructivist art education, we have seen that Vygotsky has supported collaboration, and Piaget has supported individuality in education.

Art education is an essential part of education and informs about visual literacy, critical thinking, and social justice in it. The importance of the reductive representations of innovative ideas, artistic approaches, and the production of creativity can be seen in the outcomes of aesthetics, creativity, and the process of making the artworks in traditional and nontraditional ways in art education. The implementation, interpretation, and incorporation of personal ideas can be reflected through them. Individuality often can be seen through observations, knowledge, and understanding of the process of making artworks through creativity, aesthetics, and artistic mindedness.

The process also revolves around the important parts of the history of art education through the chosen process, use of methods, materials, and functions of artworks. Visual literacy supports visual learning, visual perception, and visual understanding in education. Visual learning can make the process of teaching and learning work in it. Visual perception can support the process of learning by assessing, observing, and making decisions about the quality of artwork in it. Visual literacy can make the visual appearance, physical appearance, and visual shades of diversity understandable in it. Critical thinking is an important part of social constructivism art education. The critical thinking approach informs about critical thinking by sharing a specific point of view of a learner. Therefore, it is good to support the individual identity of each student.

Critical thinking honors individuals' identification and helps in understanding others. The information about critical thinking might minimize racism. Critical thinking helps learners think about artwork by using visual literacy in a critical way. This process requires learners to make the artwork by using their own creativity, aesthetics, and artistic skills. Artwork is also supposed to be meaningful, functional, and valuable in it. Therefore, art is supposed to be able to expand knowledge by informing about the use of a basic theme, materials, techniques, methods, and an art construction place to allow students to construct artworks by using artistic mindedness for them.

In this situation, urban art education is about diversity, equality, and inclusion in education. B.F. Skinners supports behaviorism. Behaviorism requires proper behavior from students in the classes. Students need to understand the rules and regulations to make the process work for them. By following the rules to make learnings and regulations function, students need to follow the policies to help achieve the goals through the procedures to move forward in urban education. The integration process can make the teachings work effectively by supporting, promoting, and encouraging learners for this purpose. Urban education is about diversity, equality, and inclusiveness.

I can also see that urban education talks about the issues, concerns, and outcomes of social justice to support the ethnic students that are important in the system. Each student represents personal identification as an individual in urban education. To educate ethnic students, teachers like to use their teaching methods to improve the quality of the education, curriculum, and classroom environment by making the environment inclusive and engaging for them. Educators can assess, see, explain, and evaluate the progress of the applicable policies and procedures for them. Urban education should show transparency regarding how its practices have good impacts on learners. The studies help in managing time, and developing knowledge, skills, and abilities in urban settings in urban education. The instructional lenses help keep the classroom environment more inclusive and engaging for students in urban education. Knowledge helps students in achieving goals in classes. The use of different teaching methods is expanding our knowledge. This process has always made the diverse environment of urban education more understandable for students. Visual literacy supports visual learning using visual images, visual materials, and visual scenes.

Social justice art education issues can be seen through the social dimensions, self-awareness, and the public space for them. Social justice art education is also described by Dewey in education. The process of conciliation, appeasement, and mollification is supported in the provided classes of them. I need to check the use of possible ways to adapt and find solutions through social constructivist art education. I must confirm that ethnicity does not separate learners from the diverse educational environment. I also need to ensure that the individual identification does not support racism at any level of investigation in the classes. Social justice art education supports social dimensions, self-awareness, and the public space to support the learners. The social dimensions revolve around social interactions, social practice, and social interfaces for them. Each student can use creativity, aesthetics, and personal identity to convey a message to a community.

Social interactions can help establish good relationships, and social contacts and learners can learn from each other. Social practice can provide a chance for learners to collaborate with peers, share plans, and support each other. This process also can help to support personal identities through their social practices in multiple ways. Moral support can make the learnings work effectively by letting students collaborate with a small cadre to exchange ideas, share plans, and use the chosen steps to make the process work through collaboration and so forth. The social interface can help in making an outline, working on a plan, and having a formidable team to work on the plans for them. As an individual, a student can produce different themes to represent a personal identity, individuality, and destructiveness. Aesthetics give a chance to share artistic mindedness through the chosen subject matter, cultural relevance, cultural heritage, and physical manifestation of them. To support social justice, I can see that professional education for teachers is needed to make the teachings work for learners in it. Ethnicity is an important part of the learnings in education. To support literacy, use of curriculum, and to keep students engaged, I would like to support the beauty of ethnicity for them. In the process of supporting social justice in urban art education, I would consider using social dimensions, self-awareness, and public space in it. This is also about sporting social interactions, collaboration with peers, social practice, and so forth. Having a formidable team to work on the chosen plans, I can see the importance of aesthetics to support learning by considering this process as a way to practice, use, and apply for others. Therefore, a knowledge of learners' backgrounds can help in understanding their customs, culture, traditions, values, and cultural heritage of them.

An artist's artistic mindedness through the chosen subject matter, cultural relevance, cultural heritage, and physical manifestation can be seen, felt, and observed to know more about the conveyed message through it. Multiculturalism is a part of social justice. Multiculturalism is more about the identities of the diverse community, cultural involvement, obscure, and ethereal ways to use to support it. The research is also supporting the use of social dimensions, social interactions, social engagement, social practice, social norms, and social interfaces that can make the process work in it. This will help in understanding the details of the creativeness, inspiration, and aesthetics in it. Self-awareness is a part of multiculturalism. Self-awareness can be supported through authenticity, ingenuity, civic literacy, moral ethics, and cultural heritage. The use of public space also supports multiculturalism.

Public space is about the structures so students' can share their own creativity through the physical appearance of an artwork, and interventions can also help in the functioning of an artwork by placing it at any outdoor location in the urban educational environment. Students can interact with the communities to discuss occupying a virtual space to get engaged to observe and retain in the urban environment. This process also gives a chance to learn, know, and understand the importance of the urban educational environment to impact the artists is also noticeable.

The social dimensions revolve around social interactions, social practice, and social interfaces to share their influences through their artworks. The social dimensions give a chance to students to share their creativity, artistic mindedness, and esthetics. As an individual, a student can produce different themes to support personal identity, individuality, and interactions with the community. The social dimensions also can help to support personal identity through their social practice in multiple ways. Self-awareness gives a chance to share personal choices and preferences through ingenuity. In this situation, civic literacy supports students' self-awareness, self-confidence, and self-expression by allowing them to find their own space through social justice art education.

Public space engages students by making students think about the structures, dimensions, materials, and periods also can engage students in it. Public c space gives students' a chance to share their own creativity and current concerns. Public space supports the ideas of artwork creation, and this process allows students to have conversations, communications, and interventions for this purpose. Public space includes the use of museums, galleries, and other outdoor locations for this purpose. The urban educational environment supplies a public space for students to make learning work for them, which allows students to share, inform, and interact with the communities through this process. Public space supplies a virtual space to support students for conversations, communications, and interventions to get the virtual public space experience by themselves. The use of public space engages students by making students think about the structures, dimensions, materials, and periods for engagement and awareness. Therefore, students must know and understand the use of their personal learnings to show their creativity to their teacher so they can analyze the creativity and aesthetics for them.

Teachers are also required to have enough experience to support learners in the classes. Literacy skills require enough knowledge, skills, and abilities to make the process of teaching work for them. Literacy skills also require students to learn more to expand the horizon of knowledge through practicing, learning, and making the learnings work in the classes. The use of curriculum is essential to support teaching for learners. Therefore, teachers are required to keep the classroom environment more inclusive, engaging, and innovative for learners. To keep the diverse environment more inclusive, they can use the broader spectrum of the curriculum to teach a variety of techniques by using the different methods, materials, and techniques in it. The use of a wide range of educational activities can also make the process work in these situations.

A comprehensive educational environment always makes the teachings work to support the learning work for them. To keep the educational environment of a classroom more engaging, teachers can support students so they can retain, occupy, and absorb the learnings in the same environment as their peers. To keep the classroom environment more innovative, students can be taught in an advanced, modern, and novel way to have a good impact on them. Social constructivism is informative regarding the several types of learning. The distinction between objectivity and subjectivity, communication, and pragmatic conceptions of using validity to support authenticity, legitimacy, and rationality are acceptable in qualitative research. I have observed that qualitative research supports the naturalistic world, helps in finding the solution to the issues of humans, and helps in resolving their issues in it. Therefore, researchers are able to build a holistic picture through research to find ways to support their own inquiry in education as well.

# BIOGRAPHY

Zartasha Shah is a Ph.D. student at the University of Houston main campus in Houston, Texas. She is also a researcher, artist, curator, docent, graphic designer, poet, and published writer in the United States of America. She was born and raised to the Gillani family in Bahawal Pur, Punjab, Pakistan. Now, she resides with her family in Texas, United States of America. She is married to

Syed Ahmed Shah. They have three children, including Dr. Sarosh Ahmed, Nawal Shah, and Mohammad Shah.

At the University of Houston main campus, she is studying to complete the remaining courses in the fourth year of her Ph.D. in Curriculum and Instruction with an emphasis on art education, College of Education. In the spring of 2018, she completed her MED in Curriculum and Instruction with an emphasis on art education, the College of Education, the University of Houston main campus.

In the spring of 2010, she completed her BA in Art History at the School of Art, University of Houston main campus. She has also completed a couple of certificates at the Center for the Integration of Research, Teaching, and Learning, and this includes an Associate level certificate and Partitioner level certificate at the University of Houston. At Harvard University's Graduate College of Education, she has completed a professional training course, Introduction to family engagement in education, Early childhood development global strategies for implementation, and Instructional move: making classroom discussions more inclusive and effective. At the Department of English, she has completed four certificates about Shakespeare. At Lone Star Colleges, she has completed four Associates and a couple of certificates in Texas, United States of America. She has earned 800+ points in education.

She is holding lifetime memberships of Phi Sigma Pi National Honor Fraternity, The Golden Key International Honor Society, and The National Society of Leadership and Success at the University of Houston main campus in Houston, Texas, United States. She also holding active memberships of the American Education Research Association, the National Art Education Association, The Woodlands Art League, and the Conroe Art League.

She has worked as a reviewer of AERA for the annual meetings, in Spring 2022 and 2023, and she is also accepted to review the works for 2024. As the Chair of AERA for a session, she worked in Spring 2022. As a Facilitator of AERA, she worked in Spring 2021. She has served as the Judge for the students' scholarships in Harris County and the Montgomery Country in Texas, United States. She has received several awards from Government entities, prominent individuals, and famous organizations in the United States as well as abroad.

She presented her doctoral research at the NAEA annual convention in person in NY, in the spring of 2022. She is also accepted to present her virtual research at the Information, Medium & Society: Twenty-second International Conference on Publishing Studies, at Sapienza University of Rome, Department of European, American and Intercultural Studies. This University was opened in 1303. She exhibited and curated the artworks at The Consulate General of Pakistan in Houston and the

Pakistan Center, in Houston, Texas. Some of the artworks are on a permanent display at the Consulate General of Pakistan in Houston as well. She has participated in and displayed her artwork at various locations in Texas.

Currently, she is working on a Community Outreach Program in Texas. This program is planned, presented, and applied by her. The diverse community of the country is highly appreciated by her. This program supports the customs, cultures, traditions, values, and cultural heritage of the diverse community. A large group of a diverse community is contacted to share their creativity, artistic mindedness, and aesthetics at the ten libraries of the two counties in Texas. This invitation revolves around famous celebrities from the United States as well. The program revolves around Montgomery County and Harris county so far for this purpose in it. The program will be completed in the Fall of 2023. This program is planned, presented, and applied by Zartasha Shah.

The diverse community of the country is highly appreciated by her. This program supports the customs, cultures, traditions, values, and cultural heritage of a diverse community of the country. A large group of diverse communities is contacted to share their creativity, artistic mindedness, and aesthetics at the ten libraries of the two counties in Texas. This invitation revolves around the famous celebrities of the United States as well as the board. The program revolves around Montgomery

County and Harris county for this purpose. The themes, techniques, methods, materials, and colors of the artworks can convey messages to others. They are also able to inform about the abilities, cultures, and skills of each artist in it. The majority is working perfectly in their chosen work environments, and they are also interested in the process of making the artworks to share with the diverse community of the country. This program also supports visual literacy, social engagement, public interactions, and social involvement, and provides information about the artworks of different artists that are willing to make the artworks in their own ways. This includes drawing, embroidery, painting, and photography in it.

The chosen locations for the displays are Montgomery County Central Library, George and Cynthia Woods Mitchell Library, Charles B. Stewart West Branch Library, South Regional Library, and R. B. Tullis Library in Montgomery County, Texas. In Harris county, the chosen locations are Katy Branch Library, Kingwood Branch Library, Katherine Tyre Branch, Octavia Fields Branch Library, and Clear Lake City-County Freeman Branch Library in Texas. This program gives the chance to engage, involve, and interact with the diverse community to inform, share, and get appreciation through the displays at the libraries of Montgomery county and Harris county in Texas.

She has also published a book called *Colors of Art* in

Texas. Her book is available at the Oxford University, UK, Cambridge University in the UK, and British Library in the UK as well. Her book is able circulating at the 350 libraries of Pakistan and the several libraries of the State of Texas. She has also written more than 20 articles in the different newspapers in the State of Texas. Her writing's spectrum is big and revolves around the different parts of customs, cultures, traditions, values, and the cultural heritage of the global community.

**Contact information**
zartashashah@gmail.com
zashah@uh.edu